TRAVELING LIGHT
JOURNAL

TRAVELING LIGHT
JOURNAL

WITH QUOTATIONS FROM THE BOOK BY

MAX LUCADO

W PUBLISHING GROUP™
www.wpublishinggroup.com
A Division of Thomas Nelson, Inc.
www.ThomasNelson.com

Traveling Light Journal

Compiled and edited by Karen Hill.

Produced for the W Publishing Group by The Livingstone Corporation. Project staff includes Katie Gieser, Paige Drygas, and Neil Wilson.

ISBN 0-8499-1800-6

DEDICATED TO THOSE WHO
RISKED AND LOST THEIR LIVES ON
SEPTEMBER 11, 2001

Dear Friend,

What do you do when you are hungry? When you are thirsty, how do you react? If your skin is dry, do you know how to treat it?

Of course you do. Hunger, thirst, dryness—you feed it, quench it, and moisten it. You know what to do for your body.

But what about your soul? When your heart is hungry, when your dreams are thirsty, when your spirit has run dry. Where do you turn?

I'd like to urge you to turn to your Shepherd. Jesus invites, "Come to me, all of you who are weary and carry heavy burdens, and I will give you rest" (Matthew 11:28 NLT). If you let him, your Shepherd will refresh your spirit by lightening your load—by releasing you from the burdens you were never intended to bear: burdens of worry, guilt, hopelessness, fear, shame, doubt, loneliness . . . the burdens of life.

Where do you start? A good place to begin is with the comforting, time-tested words of an old friend: the Twenty-third Psalm.

The LORD is my shepherd;
I shall not want.
He makes me to lie down in green pastures;
He leads me beside the still waters.
He restores my soul;
He leads me in the paths of righteousness
For His name's sake.

Yea, though I walk through the valley of the shadow of death,

I will fear no evil;

For You are with me;

Your rod and Your staff, they comfort me.

You prepare a table before me in the presence of my enemies;

You anoint my head with oil;

My cup runs over.

Surely goodness and mercy shall follow me

All the days of my life;

And I will dwell in the house of the LORD

Forever.

Psalm 23:1–6 NKJV

Take time to eat, drink, and be anointed by your Father. Spend a few moments every day letting him do what he wants to do: take care of you. He knows how; he is your Shepherd.

Max Lucado

This week I'll release the burden of WORRY

"Therefore do not worry about tomorrow,
for tomorrow will worry about its own things."

Matthew 6:34 NKJV

NO ONE HAS TO REMIND YOU of the high cost of anxiety. Worry divides the mind. The biblical word for *worry* (*merimnao*) is a compound of two Greek words, *merizo* (to divide) and *nous* (the mind). Anxiety splits our energy between today's priorities and tomorrow's problems. Part of our mind is on the now, the rest is on the not yet. The result is half-minded living.

That's not the only result. Worrying is not a disease, but it causes diseases. It has been connected to high blood pressure, heart trouble, blindness, migraine headaches, thyroid malfunctions, and a host of stomach disorders.

Anxiety is an expensive habit. Of course, it might be worth the cost if it worked. But it doesn't. Our frets are futile. Jesus said, "You cannot add any time to your life by worrying about it" (Matthew 6:27). Worry has never brightened a day, solved a problem, or cured a disease.

**Father, give me the courage to place in your hands
all of my worries. And give me the faith
to leave them with you.**

"Who of you by worrying
can add a single hour to his life?"

Luke 12:25 NIV

TRYING TO OVERCOME the burden of worry? There is no better place to begin than in verse two of the Twenty-third Psalm (NKJV). "He leads me beside the still waters," David declares. And, in case we missed the point, he repeats the phrase in the next verse:

"He leads me in the paths of righteousness."

"He leads me." God isn't behind me, yelling, "Go!" He is ahead of me, bidding, "Come!" He is in front, clearing the path, cutting the brush, showing the way. Just before the curve, he says, "Turn here." Prior to the rise, he motions, "Step up here." Standing next to the rocks, he warns, "Watch your step here."

He leads us. He tells us what we need to know when we need to know it.

**Lord, thank you
for being my Shepherd.
Today I'll entrust my worries to you because
I know that you will lead me.**

"Do not worry about your life, what you will eat;
or about your body, what you will wear."

Luke 12:22 NIV

WE WORRY. We worry about the IRS and the SAT and the FBI. . . .
We worry that we won't have enough money, and when we have
money we worry that we won't manage it well. We worry that the
world will end before the parking meter expires. We worry what the
dog thinks if he sees us step out of the shower. We worry that someday we'll learn that fat-free yogurt was fattening.

Honestly, now. Did God save you so you would fret? Would he
teach you to walk just to watch you fall? Would he be nailed to the
cross for your sins and then disregard your prayers? Come on. Is
Scripture teasing us when it reads, "He has put his angels in charge
of you to watch over you wherever you go" (Psalm 91:11)?

I don't think so either.

**Father, forgive me for worrying. Thank you for remind-
ing me how much you care for me and my problems.**

**Let us therefore come boldly to the throne of grace,
that we may obtain mercy and find grace to help in
time of need.**

Hebrews 4:16 NKJV

GOD'S HELP IS TIMELY. He helps us the same way a father gives plane tickets to his family. When I travel with my kids, I carry all our tickets in my satchel. When the moment comes to board the plane, I stand between the attendant and the child. As each daughter passes, I place a ticket in her hand. She, in turn, gives the ticket to the attendant. Each one receives the ticket in the nick of time.

What I do for my daughters God does for you. He places himself between you and the need. And at the right time, he gives you the ticket. This is the same promise God gave the children of Israel. He promised to supply them with manna each day. But he told them to collect only one day's supply at a time. Those who disobeyed and collected enough for two days found themselves with rotten manna. God gave them what they needed, in their time of need.

God will do the right thing at the right time. What a difference that makes.

Father, thank you for being ever present in my life.

"Give your entire attention to what God is doing right now, and don't get worked up about what may or may not happen tomorrow. God will help you deal with whatever hard things come up when the time comes."

Matthew 6:34 MSG

THAT LAST PHRASE IS WORTHY of your highlighter: "when the time comes."

"I don't know what I'll do if my husband dies." You will, *when the time comes.*

"When my children leave the house, I don't think I can take it." It won't be easy, but strength will arrive *when the time comes.*

The key is this: Meet today's problems with today's strength. Don't start tackling tomorrow's problems until tomorrow. You do not have tomorrow's strength yet. You simply have enough for today.

Lord, I need your holy strength today. Please give me what you think is best to help me face the struggles of this day.

The LORD is good, a refuge in times of trouble.
He cares for those who trust in him.

Nahum 1:7 NIV

ARTHUR HAYS SULZBERGER WAS THE publisher of the *New York Times* during the Second World War. Because of the world conflict, he found it almost impossible to sleep. He was never able to banish worries from his mind until he adopted as his motto these five words—"one step enough for me"—taken from the hymn "Lead Kindly Light":

> Lead, kindly Light . . .
>
> Keep Thou my feet; I do not ask to see
>
> The distant scene; one step enough for me.

God isn't going to let you see the distant scene either. So you might as well quit looking for it. We do not need to know what will happen tomorrow. We only need to know he leads us and "we will find grace to help us when we need it" (Hebrews 4:16 NLT).

Father, your grace truly is sufficient for me. Thank you, Gracious Lord, for watching over me and calming my anxious heart.

"So don't worry about tomorrow, because tomorrow
will have its own worries. Each day has enough trouble
of its own."

Matthew 6:34

"DON'T WORRY"? EASY TO SAY. Not always easy to do, right? We
are so prone to worry. Just last night I was worrying in my sleep. I
dreamed that I was diagnosed with ALS, a degenerative muscle disease, which took the life of my father. I awakened from the dream
and, right there in the middle of the night, began to worry. Then
Jesus' words came to my mind, "Don't worry about tomorrow." And
for once, I decided not to. I released the burden of worry. After all,
why let tomorrow's imaginary problem rob tonight's rest? Can I pre-
vent the disease by staying awake? Will I postpone the affliction by
thinking about it? Of course not. So I did the most spiritual thing I
could have done. I went back to sleep.

Why don't you do the same? God is leading you. Leave tomorrow's problems until tomorrow.

**Father, help me remember that you don't want
your children to worry, that you want me to release
the burden of worry to your tender care.**

This week
I'll release
the burden of
GUILT

He himself bore our sins in his body on the tree, so that we might die to sins and live for righteousness; by his wounds you have been healed.

1 Peter 2:24 NIV

GOD IS PLANNING A PARTY . . . a party to end all parties, in the throne room of God.

The guest list is impressive. But more impressive than the names of the guests is the nature of the guests. No egos, no power plays. Guilt, shame, and sorrow will be checked at the gate. Disease, death, and depression will be the Black Plagues of a distant past. What we now see daily, there we will never see.

And what we now see vaguely, there we will see clearly. We will see God. Not by faith. Not through the eyes of Moses or Abraham or David. Not via Scripture or sunsets or summer rains. We will see not God's work or words, but we will see him! For he is not the host of the party; he *is* the party. His goodness is the banquet. His voice is the music. His radiance is the light, and his love is the endless topic of discussion.

Father, your immeasurable gift of forgiveness brings me joy and hope. May my life prove worthy of your great sacrifice.

"God will show his mercy forever and ever to those who worship and serve him."

Luke 1:50

GOD DOES NOT SAVE US because of what we've done. Only a puny god could be bought with tithes. Only an egotistical god would be impressed with our pain. Only a temperamental god could be satisfied by sacrifices. Only a heartless god would sell salvation to the highest bidders.

And only a great God does for his children what they can't do for themselves.

God's delight is received upon surrender, not awarded upon conquest. The first step to joy is a plea for help, an acknowledgment of moral destitution, an admission of inward paucity. Those who taste God's presence have declared spiritual bankruptcy and are aware of their spiritual crisis. . . . Their pockets are empty. Their options are gone. They have long since stopped demanding justice; they are pleading for mercy.

Lord, today I surrender my life, my past, my sins to you. I am nothing without you, Father. And yet, I am everything with you. I praise your holy name for redeeming me.

13

God made him who had no sin to be sin for us, so that in him we might become the righteousness of God.

2 Corinthians 5:21 NIV

WILL GOD, WHO IS RIGHTEOUS, spend eternity with those who are not? Would Harvard admit a third-grade dropout? If it did, the act might be benevolent, but it wouldn't be right. If God accepted the unrighteous, the invitation would be even nicer, but would he be right? Would he be right to overlook our sins? Lower his standards? No. He wouldn't be right. And if God is anything, he is right.

He told Isaiah that righteousness would be his plumb line, the standard by which his house is measured (Isaiah 28:17). Or to use Paul's analogy, "We're sinners, every one of us, in the same sinking boat with everybody else." (Romans 3:19 MSG). Then what are we to do?

Carry a load of guilt? Many do. So many do.

Guilt doesn't bring us nearer to God; it distances us from him. Listen. Disappointments may discourage you. Anxiety may plague you. But guilt? Guilt consumes you.

So what do we do? Confess our need. Proclaim our guilt to the Father. And accept the righteousness of God, freely given by the One whose sacrifice makes us righteous.

Father, you are holy and righteous, and I gratefully accept your gift of redemption.

But God has a way to make people right with him.

Romans 3:21

IT WAS, AT ONCE, history's most beautiful and most horrible moment. Jesus stood in the tribunal of heaven. Sweeping a hand over all creation, he pleaded, "Punish me for their mistakes. See the murderer? Give me his penalty. The adulteress? I'll take her shame. The bigot, the liar, the thief? Do to me what you would do to them. Treat me as you would a sinner."

And God did. "For Christ died for sins once for all, the righteous for the unrighteous, to bring you to God" (1 Peter 3:18 NIV).

David said it like this: "He leads me in the paths of righteousness" (Psalm 23:3 NKJV).

The path of righteousness is a narrow, winding trail up a steep hill. At the top of the hill is a cross. At the base of the cross are bags. Countless bags full of innumerable sins. Calvary is the compost pile for guilt. Would you like to leave yours there as well?

Father, today I will transfer my burden of guilt to your loving arms. Thank you for leading me on the path of righteousness by taking my guilt.

**For all have sinned and fall short of the glory of God,
and are justified freely by his grace through the
redemption that came by Christ Jesus.**

Romans 3:23–24 NIV

WHAT IS GOD'S PERSPECTIVE ON OUR GUILT?

He doesn't condone our sin, nor does he compromise his standard.

He doesn't ignore our rebellion, nor does he relax his demands.

Rather than dismiss our sin, he assumes our sin and, incredibly, sentences himself.

God's holiness is honored. Our sin is punished . . . and we are redeemed.

God does what we cannot do so we can be what we dare not dream: perfect before God.

Does such a God want his children burdened by sin? I don't think so, either.

**Lord, thank you for reminding me to focus on your
holiness instead of my own guilt.**

Where God's love is, there is no fear, because God's perfect love drives out fear.

1 John 4:18

DO YOU HARBOR A HIDDEN FEAR that God is angry at you? Somewhere, sometime, some Sunday school class or some television show convinced you that God has a whip behind his back, a paddle in his back pocket, and he's going to nail you when you've gone too far.

No concept could be more wrong! We have a Father who is filled with compassion, a Father who hurts when his children hurt. We serve a God who says that even when we stumble, even when we disobey, he is waiting to embrace us and forgive us.

He doesn't come quarreling and wrangling and forcing his way into anyone's heart. He comes into our hearts like a gentle lamb, not a roaring lion.

Father, let me tell you what I'm feeling guilty about today . . .

17

Therefore, there is now no condemnation for those who
are in Christ Jesus . . .

Romans 8:1 NIV

IF YOU HAVE EVER WONDERED how God reacts when you fail,
frame the words [of that verse] and hang them on the wall. Read
them. . . . Ponder them. . . .

Or better still, take him with you to your canyon of shame. Invite
Christ to journey with you . . . to stand beside you as you retell the
events of the darkest nights of your soul.

And then listen. Listen carefully. He's speaking. . . . "I don't
judge you guilty."

And watch. Watch carefully. He's writing. He's leaving a message. Not in the sand, but on a cross.

Not with his hand, but with his blood.

His message has two words: not guilty.

**Father, my gratitude is limitless for the verdict you
have given me: not guilty. May my life demonstrate
my gratitude.**

This week I'll release the burden of FEAR

**Say to those with fearful hearts,
"Be strong, do not fear . . ."**

Isaiah 35:4 NIV

I'M A RUNNER. More mornings than not I drag myself out of bed and onto the street. I don't run fast. And compared to marathoners, I don't run far. But I run. I run because I don't like cardiologists. Nothing personal, mind you. It's just that I come from a family that keeps them in business. I'd like to be the one family member who doesn't keep a heart surgeon's number on speed dial.

Since heart disease runs in our family, I run in our neighborhood. And as I am running, my body is groaning. My knee hurts. My hip is stiff. My ankles complain.

Things hurt. And as things hurt, I've learned that I have three options. Go home. (My wife would laugh at me.) Meditate on my hurts until I start imagining I'm having chest pains. (Pleasant thought.) Or keep running and watch the sun come up. If I watch God's world go from dark to golden, guess what? The same happens to my attitude. The pain passes and the joints loosen, and before I know it, the run is half over and life ain't half bad. Everything improves as I fix my eyes on the sun.

Isn't the same true with your fears? If you fix your eyes on the Son, fear diminishes and trust is renewed.

Father, help me to look more to you and less to my fears.

"Father, if you are willing, take away this cup of suffering. But do what you want, not what I want."

Luke 22:42

How did Jesus endure the terror of the crucifixion? He went first to the Father with his fears. He modeled the words of Psalm 56:3: "When I am afraid, I put my trust in you" (NLT).

Do the same with yours. Don't avoid life's Gardens of Gethsemane. Enter them. Just don't enter them alone. And while there, be honest. Pounding the ground is permitted. Tears are allowed. And if you sweat blood, you won't be the first. Do what Jesus did: Open your heart.

And be specific. Jesus was. "Take *this* cup," he prayed. Give God the number of the flight. Tell him the length of the speech. Share the details of the job transfer. He has plenty of time. He also has plenty of compassion.

He doesn't think your fears are foolish or silly. He won't tell you to "buck up" or "get tough." He's been where you are. He knows how you feel.

Father, I am fearful, but I know that you are strong when I am weak. Help me sense your presence in the midst of my fear.

"May the God you serve all the time save you!"

Daniel 6:16

LOOK AT JONAH IN THE FISH BELLY—surrounded by gastric juices and sucked-seaweed. . . . He prays. . . . Before he can say amen, the belly convulses, the fish belches, and Jonah lands face first on the beach.

Look at Daniel in the lions' den; his prospects aren't much better than Jonah's. Jonah had been swallowed, and Daniel is about to be. . . .

Or look at Joseph in the pit, a chalky hole in a hot desert. The lid has been pulled over the top and the wool has been pulled over his eyes. . . . Like Jonah and Daniel, Joseph is trapped. He is out of options. There is no exit. There is no hope. . . . Though the road to the palace takes a detour through a prison, it eventually ends up at the throne. . . .

Such are the stories in the Bible. One near-death experience after another. Just when the neck is on the chopping block, just when the noose is around the neck, Calvary comes.

Lord, thank you for being my rescuer. Thank you for the assurance that you are watchful, that you care, and that you are my protector.

[Jesus] began to be troubled and deeply distressed.

Mark 14:33 NKJV

WHAT DO YOU FEAR? Boarding an airplane? Facing a crowd? Public speaking? Taking a job? Taking a spouse? Driving on a highway? The source of your fear may seem small to others. But to you, it freezes your feet, makes your heart pound, and brings blood to your face. That's what happened to Jesus.

Jesus was more than anxious; he was afraid. . . . How remarkable that Jesus felt such fear. But how kind that he told us about it. We tend to do the opposite. Gloss over our fears. Cover them up. Keep our sweaty palms in our pockets, our nausea and dry mouths a secret. Not so with Jesus. We see no mask of strength. But we do hear a request for strength.

"Father, if you are willing, take away this cup of suffering." The first one to hear his fear is his Father. He could have gone to his mother. He could have confided in his disciples. He could have assembled a prayer meeting. All would have been appropriate, but none were his priority. He went first to his father.

Father, when I'm afraid, I will trust in you.

Surely God is my salvation;
I will trust and not be afraid.

Isaiah 12:2 NIV

GOD UNDERSTANDS YOUR FEARS. He knows what you need. That's why we punctuate our prayers as Jesus did. "If you are willing . . ."

Was God willing? Yes and no. He didn't take away the cross, but he took the fear. God didn't still the storm, but he calmed the sailor.

Who's to say he won't do the same for you?

"Do not be anxious about anything, but in everything, by prayer and petition, with thanksgiving, present your requests to God" (Philippians 4:6 NIV).

Don't measure the size of the mountain; talk to the One who can move it. Instead of carrying the world on your shoulders, talk to the One who holds the universe on his. Hope is a look away.

Father, I'm looking to you and asking you to calm
my fears, trusting that you will do what is best and
what is right.

The One who died for us . . . is in the presence of God at this very moment sticking up for us.

Romans 8:34 MSG

JESUS IS PRAYING FOR US. . . . Jesus has spoken and Satan has listened. The devil may land a punch or two. He may even win a few rounds, but he never wins the fight. Why? Because Jesus takes up for you. . . . "So he is able always to save those who come to God through him because he always lives, asking God to help them" (Hebrews 7:25).

Jesus, at this very moment, is protecting you. . . . Evil must pass through Christ before it can touch you. And God will "never let you be pushed past your limit; he'll always be there to help you come through it" (1 Corinthians 10:13 MSG).

Just knowing that helps dispel fear, doesn't it?

Lord, thank you for bringing calm to the storms of my fears.

The Father has loved us so much that we are called children of God. And we really are his children.

1 John 3:1

Do YOU FEAR that you're not "good enough" for God? Let me tell you just who you are. In fact, let me proclaim who you are.

You are an heir of God and a co-heir with Christ (Romans 8:17).

You are eternal, like an angel (Luke 20:36).

You have a crown that will last forever (1 Corinthians 9:25).

You are a holy priest (1 Peter 2:5), a treasured possession (Exodus 19:5).

But more than any of the above—more significant than any other title or position—is the simple fact that you are God's child.

"We really are his children."

Now, what were you saying?

Father, you are my Father, and I will not fear. I know that nothing can separate me from you, and that fact brings great peace.

This week
I'll release
the burden of
LONELINESS

You are with me.

Psalm 23:4 NKJV

COULD IT BE THAT LONELINESS is not a curse but a gift? A gift from God?

Wait a minute, Max. That can't be. Loneliness heavies my heart. Loneliness leaves me empty and depressed. Loneliness is anything but a gift.

But could it be that loneliness is God's way of getting our attention?

He would do that? Absolutely. "The Lord disciplines those he loves" (Hebrews 12:6). If he must silence every voice, he will. He wants you to hear his voice. He wants you to discover what David discovered and to be able to say what David said.

"You are with me."

Yes, you, Lord, are in heaven. Yes, you rule the universe. Yes, you sit upon the stars and make your home in the deep. But yes, yes, yes, you are with me.

**Father, when I feel lonely, remind me of your presence.
Let me know that you are with me.**

Jesus replied, "If anyone loves me, he will obey my teaching. My Father will love him, and we will come to him and make our home with him."

John 14:23 NIV

THE LORD IS WITH ME. The Creator is with me. Yahweh is with me.

Moses proclaimed it: "What great nation has a god as near to them as the LORD our God is near to us?" (Deuteronomy 4:7 NLT).

Paul announced it: "He is not far from each one of us" (Acts 17:27 NIV).

And David discovered it: "You are with me" (Psalm 23:4 NKJV).

Somewhere in the pasture, wilderness, or palace, David discovered that God meant business when he said:

"I will not leave you" (Genesis 28:15).

"I will . . . not forsake My people" (1 Kings 6:13 NKJV).

"The LORD will not abandon His people" (Psalm 94:14 NASB).

"God . . . will never leave you nor forsake you" (Deuteronomy 31:6 NIV).

The discovery of David is indeed the message of Scripture—*the Lord is with us.* And, since the Lord is near, everything is different. Everything!

Lord, be near to me today! I give you this day and rejoice in your promise to make my heart your home.

Be still before the LORD and wait patiently for him.

Psalm 37:7 NIV

IS THIS A SEASON of solitude for you? Do the days ahead echo with loneliness? Then remember that God is with you.

You may be facing death, but you aren't facing death alone; the Lord is with you. You may be facing unemployment, but you aren't facing unemployment alone; the Lord is with you. You may be facing marital struggles, but you aren't facing them alone; the Lord is with you. You may be facing debt, but you aren't facing debt alone; the Lord is with you.

Underline these words: You are not alone.

Your family may turn against you, but God won't. Your friends may betray you, but God won't. You may feel alone in the wilderness, but you are not. He is with you. And because he is, everything is different. *You* are different.

God changes your *n* into a *v*. You go from *lonely* to *lovely*.

Father, your presence enriches my days. Thank you for walking with me through the lonely times of life.

Delight yourself in the LORD and he will give you the desires of your heart.

Psalm 37:4 NIV

WHEN YOU KNOW GOD LOVES YOU, you won't be desperate for the love of others.

You'll no longer be a hungry shopper at the market. Have you ever gone to the grocery on an empty stomach? You're a sitting duck. You buy everything you don't need. Doesn't matter if it is good for you—you just want to fill your tummy. When you're lonely, you do the same in life, pulling stuff off the shelf, not because you need it, but because you are hungry for love.

Why do we do it? Because we fear facing life alone. For fear of not fitting in, we take the drugs. For fear of standing out, we wear the clothes. For fear of appearing small, we go into debt and buy the house. For fear of going unnoticed, we dress to seduce or to impress. For fear of sleeping alone, we sleep with anyone. For fear of not being loved, we search for love in all the wrong places.

But all that changes when we discover God's perfect love. And "perfect love casts out fear" (1 John 4:18 NKJV).

Father, help me understand and accept that a lonely season can bring me closer to you.

Give ear to my words, O LORD,

consider my sighing.

Listen to my cry for help,

my King and my God,

for to you I pray.

Psalm 5:1–2 NIV

LONELINESS IS NOT THE ABSENCE OF FACES. It is the absence
of intimacy. Loneliness doesn't come from being alone; it comes
from feeling alone. Feeling as if you are facing death alone, facing
disease alone, facing the future alone.

Whether it strikes you in your bed at night or on your drive to
the hospital, in the silence of an empty house or in the noise of a
crowded bar, loneliness is when you think, *I feel so alone. Does anyone
care?*

Loneliness is a burden we would gladly give up. Bags of loneliness show up everywhere. They litter the floors of boardrooms and
clubs. We drag them into parties and usually drag them back out.
You'll spot them near the desk of the overworker, beside the table of
the overeater, and on the nightstand of the one-night stand. We'll try
anything to unload our loneliness. This is one bag we want to drop
quickly.

Where will you turn for help?

Father, when a winter of loneliness comes,

I ask you to give me the warmth of your presence.

We belong to him;
we are his people, the sheep he tends.

Psalm 100:3

EACH OF US HAS A FANTASY that our family will be like the Waltons, an expectation that our dearest friends will be our next of kin. Jesus didn't have that expectation. When Jesus' brothers didn't share his convictions, he didn't try to force them. He recognized that his spiritual family could provide what his physical family didn't. . . .

We can't control the way our family responds to us. Sometimes family can be the greatest source of loneliness. When it comes to the behavior of others toward us, our hands are tied. We have to move beyond the naive expectation that if we do good, people will treat us right. The fact is they may and they may not—we cannot control how people respond to us. . . .

Let God give you what your family doesn't. If your earthly father doesn't affirm you, then let your heavenly Father take his place.

Father, thank you for being my Father, and for
loving and comforting me.

**Faith means . . . knowing that something is real
even if we do not see it.**

Hebrews 11:1

So you think you're alone? You think no one cares or no one
notices?

Someday, when you reach eternity, you may be surprised to learn
that you were never alone. God has been with you all the way. Oh,
sometimes you hardly noticed. Only when you get home will you
know how many times he protected you. Only eternity will reveal the
time he:

Interfered with the transfer, protecting you from involvement in
unethical business;

Fogged in the airport, distancing you from a shady opportunity;

Flattened your tire, preventing you from checking into the hotel
and meeting a seductive man;

Placed the right voice with the right message on the right radio
station the day you needed his encouragement.

Are you sure you're alone?

**Father, help me trust you more to watch over me when
I'm feeling alone. And thank you for all the days you
stepped into my life, without my even knowing.**

Conclusion

You've come to the end of this four-week journal of faith, but I trust it's merely the beginning of your journey. As you meet your Shepherd, let him renew and refresh your spirit.

I pray that you've left some of your burdens at the foot of the cross.

And remember: Regardless of the challenges of life, there is One who cares and will never leave you.

"We are his people, the sheep he tends" (Psalm 100:3).

*The LORD is my
shepherd;
I shall not want.*

PSALM 23:1 NKJV

He makes me to lie down in green pastures.

Psalm 23:2 NKJV

He leads me beside the still waters.

Psalm 23:2 NKJV

*He restores my
soul.*

PSALM 23:3 NKJV

He leads me in the paths of righteousness for His name's sake.

Psalm 23:3 NKJV

*Yea,
though I walk
through
the valley of the
shadow of death,
I will
fear no evil.*

PSALM 23:4 NKJV

*For You are with
me; Your rod
and Your staff,
they comfort me.*

PSALM 23:4 NKJV

*You prepare a
table before me
in the presence
of my enemies.*

PSALM 23:5 NKJV

*My cup
runs over.*

PSALM 23:5 NKJV

*Through the
LORD's mercies
we are not
consumed,
because His
compassions
fail not.*

LAMENTATIONS 3:22 NKJV

*Surely goodness
and mercy shall
follow me all the
days of my life.*

PSALM 23:6 NKJV

*I will dwell in
the house of the
LORD forever.*

PSALM 23:6 NKJV

*"Therefore, do
not worry about
tomorrow, for
tomorrow will
worry about its
own things."*

Matthew 6:34 NKJV

*"Who of you by
worrying can
add a single
hour to his life?"*

Luke 12:25 NIV

*"Do not worry
about your life,
what you will
eat; or about
your body, what
you will wear."*

Luke 12:22 niv

The Lord is good, a refuge in times of trouble. He cares for those who trust in him.

Nahum 1:7 niv

"God will show his mercy forever and ever to those who worship and serve him."

LUKE 1:50

*God has a way
to make people
right with him.*

Romans 3:21

_Where God's
love is, there is
no fear, because
God's perfect
love drives out
fear._

1 JOHN 4:18

Therefore, there is now no condemnation for those who are in Christ Jesus.

ROMANS 8:1 NIV

Say to those with fearful hearts, "Be strong, do not fear."

ISAIAH 35:4 NIV

*Surely God is my
salvation;
I will trust and
not be afraid.*

Isaiah 12:2 NIV

The Father has loved us so much that we are called children of God. And we really are his children.

1 JOHN 3:1

Delight yourself in the LORD and he will give you the desires of your heart.

PSALM 37:4 NIV

We belong to him; we are his people, the sheep he tends.

PSALM 100:3

The LORD is my shepherd;
I shall not want.

PSALM 23:1 NKJV

*He makes me to
lie down in
green pastures.*

PSALM 23:2 NKJV

He leads me beside the still waters.

Psalm 23:2 NKJV

He restores my soul.

PSALM 23:3 NKJV

*He leads me in
the paths of
righteousness for
His name's sake.*

PSALM 23:3 NKJV

*Yea,
though I walk
through
the valley of the
shadow of death,
I will
fear no evil.*

PSALM 23:4 NKJV

For You are with me; Your rod and Your staff, they comfort me.

PSALM 23:4 NKJV

*You prepare a
table before me
in the presence
of my enemies.*

PSALM 23:5 NKJV

*My cup
runs over.*

PSALM 23:5 NKJV

*Through the
LORD's mercies
we are not
consumed,
because His
compassions
fail not.*

LAMENTATIONS 3:22 NKJV

*Surely goodness
and mercy shall
follow me all the
days of my life.*

PSALM 23:6 NKJV

*I will dwell in
the house of the
LORD forever.*

PSALM 23:6 NKJV

*"Therefore, do
not worry about
tomorrow, for
tomorrow will
worry about its
own things."*

MATTHEW 6:34 NKJV

> *"Who of you by worrying can add a single hour to his life?"*
>
> LUKE 12:25 NIV

*"Do not worry
about your life,
what you will
eat; or about
your body, what
you will wear."*

Luke 12:22 NIV

> *The LORD is good,*
> *a refuge in times*
> *of trouble.*
> *He cares for*
> *those who trust*
> *in him.*
>
> NAHUM 1:7 NIV

> *"God will show his mercy forever and ever to those who worship and serve him."*
>
> LUKE 1:50

*God has a way
to make people
right with him.*

ROMANS 3:21

Where God's love is, there is no fear, because God's perfect love drives out fear.

1 JOHN 4:18

Therefore, there is now no condemnation for those who are in Christ Jesus.

ROMANS 8:1 NIV

Say to those with fearful hearts, "Be strong, do not fear."

Isaiah 35:4 NIV

*Surely God is my
salvation;
I will trust and
not be afraid.*

Isaiah 12:2 niv

> The Father
> has loved us
> so much that
> we are called
> children of God.
> And we
> really are his
> children.
>
> 1 JOHN 3:1

*Delight yourself
in the LORD and
he will give you
the desires of
your heart.*

PSALM 37:4 NIV

We belong to him; we are his people, the sheep he tends.

PSALM 100:3

*The LORD is my
shepherd;
I shall not want.*

PSALM 23:1 NKJV